The Kingdom of Yugoslavia: The Turbulent History of the Country's Formation and Occupation during World War I and World War II

By Charles River Editors

The flag of Yugoslavia

About Charles River Editors

Charles River Editors is a boutique digital publishing company, specializing in bringing history back to life with educational and engaging books on a wide range of topics. Keep up to date with our new and free offerings with this 5 second sign up on our weekly mailing list, and visit Our Kindle Author Page to see other recently published Kindle titles.

We make these books for you and always want to know our readers' opinions, so we encourage you to leave reviews and look forward to publishing new and exciting titles each week.

Introduction

Marshal Tito and Eleanor Roosevelt

The Kingdom of Yugoslavia

"No country of people's democracy has so many nationalities as this country has. Only in Czechoslovakia do there exist two kindred nationalities, while in some of the other countries there are only minorities. Consequently in these countries of people's democracy there has been no need to settle such serious problems as we have had to settle here. With them the road to socialism is less complicated than is the case here. With them the basic factor is the class issue, with us it is both the nationalities and the class issue. The reason why we were able to settle the nationalities question so thoroughly is to be found in the fact that it had begun to be settled in a revolutionary way in the course of the Liberation War, in which all the nationalities in the country participated, in which every national group made its contribution to the general effort of liberation from the occupier according to its capabilities. Neither the Macedonians nor any other national group which until then had been oppressed obtained their national liberation by decree. They fought for their national liberation with rifle in hand. The role of the Communist Party lay in the first place in the fact that it led that struggle, which was a guarantee that after the war the national question would be settled decisively in the way the communists had conceived long before the war and during the war. The role of the Communist Party in this respect today, in the phase of building socialism, lies in making the positive national factors a stimulus to, not a brake on, the development of socialism in our country. The role of the Communist Party today lies in the necessity for keeping a sharp lookout to see that national chauvinism does not appear and develop among any of the nationalities. The Communist Party must always endeavour, and does endeavour, to ensure that all the negative phenomena of nationalism disappear and that people are educated in the spirit of internationalism." - Tito

Yugoslavia was arguably one of the most unusual geopolitical creations of the 20th century. The Yugoslav state had never existed in any historical sense, and the ties that bound together its constituent peoples were tenuous at best. Although nominally all "Slavs," the country was an amalgamation of languages, alphabets, cultures, religions and traditions, which ensured its short existence was littered with splits, conflicts, and shocking violence. In a sense, it's somewhat surprising that it lasted as long as it did.

In the wake of World War I, as the political boundaries of Europe and the Middle East were redrawn, the Kingdom of Yugoslavia, initially known as the Kingdom of Serbs, Croats and Slovenes, came into existence with a monarch as its head of state. Confirmed at the 1919 Versailles Conference, the "first" Yugoslavia was a particularly fragile enterprise, and there was almost constant tension between the majority Serbs and the other Yugoslav nationalities, especially the Croats. As a result, the Kingdom was a land of political assassinations, underground terrorist organizations, and ethnic animosities. In 1929, King Alexander I suspended democracy and ruled as a dictator until he himself was assassinated in 1934.

The Kingdom of Yugoslavia was particularly vulnerable to the forces that engulfed the rest of Europe at the end of the 1930s, including fascism and communism. When the Axis forces attacked in 1941, the country quickly capitulated and was dismembered by the Nazis and their allies. A separate Croatian state was formed, led by Ante Pavelić, who committed some of the worst crimes and human rights abuses of the war. The Balkan region was virtually emptied of its Jewish population, victims of the Nazi Holocaust.

From the beginning, fascism was opposed by two major groups in the region, the monarchist Chetniks and the communist Partisans. The latter, led by Josip Broz Tito and backed by the democratic powers, emerged in the dominant position at the end of the war. The World War II era produced many leaders of titanic determination, men whose strengths and weaknesses left an extraordinary imprint on historical affairs, and the struggle between massively divergent ideologies catapulted some individuals unexpectedly onto the world stage. Marshal Tito was undoubtedly one of these figures. Originally a machinist, Tito leveraged his success in the Communist Party of Yugoslavia (CPY) and a number of extraordinary strokes of luck into dictatorial rule over Yugoslavia for a span of 35 years. World War II proved the watershed that enabled him to secure control of the country, leading an ever more powerful army of communist partisans against both the Germans and other Yugoslav factions. During the war, SS leader Heinrich Himmler himself begrudgingly stated, "He has really earned his title of Marshal. When we catch him we shall kill him at once...but I wish we had a dozen Titos in Germany, men who were leaders and had such resolution and good nerves, that, even though they were forever encircled, they would never give in.

During his reign, Tito managed to quash the intense national feelings of the diverse groups making up the Yugoslavian population, and he did so through several methods. He managed to successfully play the two superpower rivals, the United States and Soviet Union, off against each other during the Cold War, and in doing so, he maintained a considerable amount of independence from both, even as he additionally received foreign aid to keep his regime afloat. All the while he remained defiant, once penning a legendary letter to Joseph Stalin warning the Soviet dictator, "To Joseph Stalin: Stop sending people to kill me! We've already captured five of them, one of them with a bomb and another with a rifle... If you don't stop sending killers, I'll send a very fast working one to Moscow and I certainly won't have to send another."

Never afraid to use political murder when expedient, yet simultaneously outgoing and good-humored to those around him, Tito created a unique and unusual state between the Western democracies and the Eastern Bloc. Only upon his death did the fabric of the state tear asunder and age-old identities reassert themselves, bringing about a period of intense conflicts that produced a new equilibrium with ethnically-based successor states that cracked up the state he once led. Cold War rivalries also provided Yugoslavia with a geopolitical significance that evaporated after the fall of the Berlin Wall. Without its charismatic dictator who transcended national rivalries and two superpowers interested in its stability, Yugoslavia collapsed within the space of a few short, bloody years in the 1990s.

The Kingdom of Yugoslavia: The Turbulent History of the Country's Formation and Occupation during World War I and World War II examines how the multicultural nation was founded, the inherent tensions there, and the effects of the Axis occupation during World War II. Along with pictures of important people and places, you will learn about the Kingdom of Yugoslavia like never before.

The Kingdom of Yugoslavia: The Turbulent History of the Country's Formation and Occupation during World War I and World War II

The Balkans' Different Ethnic Identities

"If you humble yourself too much, you will get trampled on." – Ancient Serbian proverb

Though the Turkish persecution of the Serbians under the Ottoman Empire is a part of Serbian history that is often swept under the rug, their descendants never forgot the seemingly endless trials of their ancestors. The Muslim Turkish rulers not only set out to erase the Serbian social elite, they were determined to sever the Orthodox Christian roots its population desperately clung to. Those who could afford it fled to neighboring nations for refuge, while the rest were ejected from their rightful lands, left with no choice but to set up camp in "hostile mountains."

The homes and properties of all Orthodox Christian Serbians were promptly confiscated by Turkish authorities, and the bulk of the people were unwillingly tethered to a system of serfdom under their foreign masters, otherwise known as the "*giours.*" Their new subjects, the Serbian masses, were derogatorily referred to as the "*rayah,*" meaning "the herd." Even worse were the suffocating laws that singled out the Christian Serbs. They were only to possess mules, leaving horses, camels, and other "superior" means of travel for Turkish and Muslim use. On that note, they were never to ride a mule in the presence of a Muslim, nor could they own houses or other property that would outshine a Turkish abode. Fantastic churches and *rayah* buildings were torn down in droves, and what was left of them in pitiful conditions at best, their church bells rusting over from neglect. Needless to say, erecting new ones was out of the question. The *Rayah* were forbidden from burying their dead in broad daylight, nor could they utter the name of Christ in the presence of a Muslim.

Turkish sultans kidnapped generations of Christian Serbian children – some say up to 5 million – to equip their slave-fueled Janissary armies under a system called the "*devsirme*." Authorities whipped these boys into shape, and exploiting their Stockholm syndromes, implanted in their young minds a ride-or-die loyalty for their captors. Many Ottomans abused their privileged positions, the worst of them employing the *jus primae noctis*, or the "right of the first night." Plainly put, Turkish men were granted first dibs on Serbian servant women on their wedding nights, a humiliating practice that carried on until the 19th century. The list of injustices seemed to stretch on for miles.

There existed a door that guaranteed one access to a much brighter future, but like most entries, it came attached with a price of admission. A Serbian had to formally renounce their Christian faiths and embrace the Ottoman brand of Islam. Only then would the rights of a "full citizen" be bestowed upon them. Many struggled at the crossroads. Some, fretting over the futures of their loved ones, made the tentative step over the line, whereas most refused to budge, digging their heels into the ground.

The early 1800s brought about the first wave of Serbian insurgencies. The Serbians rejoiced as the revolutionary leader, a ferocious man known only as Karađorđe ("Black George"), took matters into his own hands and beheaded the quartet of Janissaries previously heading Serbia, relieving the people from the crush of their heels. By December 1806, Karađorđe and his troops had seized Belgrade, soon to become its capital.

Karađorđe

For the next 7 years, the Serbians ran their own ship, giving them their first, albeit fleeting, taste of freedom. Karađorđe was named the Grand Vožd of Serbia, and in 1808, a constitution of Serbia's own was published. Not only did Christian churches appear again, a string of Serbian schools were established in Belgrade, one of which eventually blossomed into a prestigious university.

By October 1813, however, Turkish soldiers swarmed into Serbia once more, replanting their flags in Belgrade in short order. As the story goes, Turkish authorities, infuriated by the Serbians' insubordination, allowed their soldiers to slay any Serbian over the age of 15 and enslave as many maidens and children as they could get their hands on for a period of two weeks. Up to 1,800 Serbian slaves were sold in a day.

Rather than submit to the Ottomans, the Serbian hunger for independence only grew more powerful. While much of their physical culture had been destroyed by their oppressors, subsisting only on a few epic poems about Serbian victories on the battlefield and the like, the Serbian spirit had not lost its character. The Serbian community not only held strong to their Orthodox Christian beliefs and distinctive cultural traits, their increasing exposure to foreign democracies continued to fan the flames of their patriotism.

Merchants who journeyed to Habsburg-operated Hungary with stacks of plump, acorn-fed pork in their wagons were some of the first to dip their toes into the light at the end of the tunnel. This was a place that treated Christians – albeit German Catholics – with due respect, and it appeared to accept the Orthodox Serbian neighbors with little to no hesitation. A few Serbians even held posts in Hungarian administrative offices and enlisted for the Austrian side during the Austro-Turkish War. It was here that they picked up on Hungarian military tactics and organizational skills that allowed them to secure their seven year spell of independence. They also found a father figure of sorts in Russia, for this modern "Slavic and Orthodox country" had become a formidable threat to the Ottomans.

More Serbians began to chase trade and educational opportunities beyond the border, and as such, they explored unfamiliar, but groundbreaking schools of thought in regards to philosophy, law, politics, and societal values shaped by rationalist and romanticist ideals. Serbian scholars left and right attempted to revitalize the local culture. Dositej Obradovic, a traveling monk, not only translated a number of foreign texts, he spun together a series of dictionaries and grammatical textbooks penned in the modern Serbian tongue. Another Enlightenment-era wordsmith, Vuk Karadzic, churned out collections of epic poetry dedicated to Serbian identity, many of its values sympathizing with the peasant communities.

By 1867, the Principality of Serbia would be awarded some semblance of independence, but the 1878 Congress of Berlin cemented the Austrian administration's position behind the scenes. Many, particularly the peasant and newly-enlightened masses, saw this not only as a stall in progress – to subject themselves to outside authority would mean taking a tremendous step backwards. It would not be long before their suspicions were realized, for Serbian conservatives, many of them supposedly puppets of the Austrians, began to drive a rift between the local patrician and plebeian classes. Only Serbian elites were inducted to civil office and awarded privileges the peasant classes were robbed of, for the plebeians were deemed too uneducated and incompetent to handle governmental affairs. What was more, the voices of the peasantry were often silenced; those who spoke out against the government were immediately tossed behind bars on the charge of public disobedience.

Belgrade pulsed with the cries of liberal university students who sided with the plebeians, many lambasting the conservatives for their "draconian legislation and hollow...corrupt system of administration." The discontent among the masses continued to swell, spawning an epidemic of overzealous, fanatical nationalism. This phenomenon was anything but lost on one notorious underground syndicate known as the "Black Hand," which would capitalize on these feelings of frustration and resentment to push for the creation of a Greater Serbia. So potent was their vision that they were willing to go to any extreme to secure it.

In order to fully understand the implications and motivation for the Black Hand's actions, it's necessary to understand the situation in Serbia and the Balkans as a whole, and why a small region whose chief importance in the previous centuries had been as a battleground for the great powers to control access to Europe became responsible for the outbreak of World War I. Three years after Archduke Franz Ferdinand's birth, in 1878, the Great Powers signed the Treaty of Berlin, a document intended to pacify the Balkans, where the Ottoman Empire had been forced to use brutal force to suppress rebellion on more than one recent occasion. Among other clauses, the Treaty empowered the Austro-Hungarian Empire to take nominal charge of the Bosnia District of the Ottoman Empire, although it officially remained Turkish territory. At the same time, the Treaty also acknowledged the sovereignty of the Principality (later the Kingdom) of Serbia, under the aegis of King Milan Obrenovic, whose family was closely connected to Emperor Franz Joseph's and was well-liked at court. This diplomatic connection helped ensure stability within a notoriously volatile region; administrative power passing to a European power with a Christian government and a long-term vested interest in the East helped quell much of the turmoil to which the Balkans had been subject to under Ottoman rule, while Serbia provided a useful and friendly bulwark to calm any unrest which might occur.

The tension in the Balkans was symptomatic of what was occurring in Europe as a whole. In the briefest of terms, by 1900 there existed in Europe an interconnected series of alliances, treaties and pacts, both overt and secret, that were intended to maintain the balance of power and the status quo on the mainland, the likes of which had never been seen before. The purpose of this web of alliances was ostensibly to ensure peace, but in reality it meant that an aggressive power could wage small-scale wars with virtual impunity thanks to the looming threat of a full-scale escalation on the European mainland, as had occurred during the Schleiswig-Holstein Question and the Franco-Prussian War (both conflicts started by what was now Germany).

The first of these alliances emerged in the wake of the Napoleonic Wars with the creation of the Holy Alliance, a "triumvirate" of Austria, Russia and Prussia. 60 years later, Otto von Bismarck, perhaps the greatest politician of his age (and certainly the most effective champion of the Prussian cause), created the *dreikaiserbund*, the League of the Three Caesars, a re-affirmation of the previous alliance renegotiated to include Germany. Fittingly, this alliance fell apart over the Balkans, as Russia and Austria-Hungary were at odds over how to administer and exert influence across the region. Thus, in 1879, Germany and Austria-Hungary dropped Russia as a partner to form the Dual Alliance, and three years later, Austria set aside its differences with Italy, which had recently fought two viciously contested wars of independence against Austria to achieve sovereignty. Together, these three nations formed the Triple Alliance.

Bismarck

Things held together (albeit in an extremely fragile fashion) until roughly 1890, shortly after the ascension to the throne of Germany of Kaiser Wilhelm II. Wilhelm was concerned about the vast and shadowy power still wielded by Bismarck, so he compelled Bismarck to resign out of fear that he would undermine the legitimacy and power of the German monarchy by being the de facto ruler. This was a legitimate fear given that the diplomatic circles of Europe still contacted Bismarck over matters of international policy thanks to their decades-long familiarity with him. What Wilhelm failed to take into account was just how much Bismarck had wielded his personality, ruthlessness, personal magnetism and sheer diplomatic brilliance to keep Germany safe and ensure its constant expansion despite the minefield of European politics. With Bismarck gone, the fragile, informal diplomatic ties he had maintained disintegrated, and in 1890 the Kaiser committed a serious political blunder by refusing to renew the Re-Insurance Treaty, which guaranteed mutual non-aggression between Russia and Germany. Russia then went on to sign the Franco-Russian Alliance with France in 1902, effectively hemming in Germany between two largely hostile powers. France also signed a treaty with Britain, the Entente Cordiale, and in 1907 Britain involved itself further in European affairs by signing the Anglo-Russian Convention. These were not formal alliances, but for simplicity's sake, this complex Anglo-Russian-French arrangement is usually referred to as the Triple Entente. While there were no formal guarantees that Britain would intervene if either France or Russia were attacked or went to war, they certainly strengthened the possibility that this would occur.

Matters in Europe were further complicated by the massive escalation of an arms race. In the wake of the Franco-Prussian War of 1871, Germany had established itself as the dominant power in Europe, and German industrial output had grown by orders of magnitude. By the dawn of the 20th century, Germany was even competing with the mighty Royal Navy for domain over the world's oceans, an impressive output for a country that had never truly made naval power a priority. The *Kaiserliche Marine*, with its modern destroyers, worried the British so much that in 1906 they launched HMS *Dreadnought*, the most powerful battleship of its time. This race for technological supremacy was as much saber-rattling as it was a genuine policy to ensure sufficiently modern equipment in fear of an attack by another European great power, but regardless, military spending almost doubled among most of the powerful nations. Moreover, virtually all nations adopted new breech-loading bolt-action rifles to go along with new artillery pieces, heavy and super-heavy mortars and railway guns, machine guns, grenades, poison gas shells, and a host of other instruments of destruction. As a result, weapons were becoming deadlier and more powerful just as nations like Germany and Italy were following burgeoning imperialistic agendas, and just as the British and French sought to prevent their expansion.

Nevertheless, the creation of Yugoslavia long predates the Cold War. It was a creature of the post-World War One settlement and of the Versailles Conference.[1] The country consistently lacked popular legitimacy, including during its first phase. The various component nationalities were suspicious of one another, particularly the smaller nations towards the majority Serbs. It is worth considering how the state of Yugoslavia came about at all. The answer lies in the particular confluence of geopolitics – the collapse of two huge empires, Austro-Hungary and the Ottomans – as well as a small but committed group of proponents. Crucially, during the First World War between 1914 and 1918, the Allied Great Powers - Britain, France and the United States – all quiesced to the foundation of Yugoslavia, or the Kingdom of Serbs, Croats and Slovenes.

Turmoil Before World War I

The Balkan area has historically been one of the world's most combustible regions. Home to several national groups and at a crossroads of Europe, Asia and the Middle East, the Balkans have exerted an outsized role on world affairs. Infamously, the assassination of Austrian

---

[1] Dejan Djokić, *Pašić & Trumbić: The Kingdom of Serbs, Croats and Slovenes.* (Haus Publishing, 2010)

Archduke Franz Ferdinand by a Serb nationalist, Gavrilo Princip, caused the dominoes to fall, leading to the First World War.

The Balkans, however, had been flammable long before Princip's bullets murdered the Austrian monarch-in-waiting. A number of countries had attempted to expand their borders within the Balkan region, and many of these had been supported by larger continental powers, such as Russia, Britain, France, Austria, Germany, and Italy. The main cause of this instability was the decline of empire in the Balkans; the Ottoman Empire had held sway over the southeast section of the Balkans since the 15th century, while the Austrian Habsburgs were dominant in the northwest of the region. Both empires moved into relative decline in the 19th century, albeit in different ways. The Ottoman territories were slowly lost to other encroaching forces, while the Austrians (and then Austro-Hungarians) actually expanded until the First World War. This turned out to be a case of "imperial overstretch," and as the two hegemons weakened, a number of political spaces opened up. The wake of World War I would produce a nation made up of Serbs, Croats, Bosnians, Slovenes, Macedonians, and Montenegrins. These nationalities, however, would not prove satisfactory for many in the new country, and others would later emerge, most notably the Kosovan Albanians and Bosniaks.

In addition to the nationalities that would be part of Yugoslavia, the Balkans was home to a number of other identities, ethnicities, and traditions, and the Greeks, Bulgarians, Romanians, Albanians and Turks would all play a role in the development of Yugoslavia as well.

As mentioned earlier, the Serbs had shown themselves to be potent adversaries in the Balkan region and prized themselves as warriors. Notions of a Serb-nation focused on the 1389 "Battle of Kosovo," on the "Field of Blackbirds," where the Ottomans had defeated a Serb army but nevertheless gave Serbia a sense of identity in a hostile region. Kosovo also became an integral part of any notion of a Serb state. As a predominantly Christian Orthodox people, Serbia also gained fraternal support from co-religionists, most notably Russia.

Croatia was the second largest of the Yugoslav nations. Croats were Catholic and saw themselves as more inherently part of European "civilization" compared to the other Yugoslav nationalities, though it should be noted that this sentiment was shared by most of the Slavic ethnicities. The region that incorporates modern Croatia was part of the Austrian Habsburg Empire for several centuries and gained some autonomy in 1868. Croatian nationalism had grown during the century, and a number of groups were agitating for full independence during the First World War.

Bosnia, meanwhile, was a more complicated area. Home to large minorities of self-described ethnic Serbs and Croats, the majority of Bosnians were Muslim, sometimes (later) known as Bosnian Muslims or Bosniaks. Bosnians had lived in the territory for centuries but enjoyed some preferential treatment under the Islamic Ottoman Empire. Nevertheless, a specific version of Bosnian nationalism grew during the 19th century, and the country – known as Bosnia and

Herzegovina – was occupied by Austria-Hungary from 1878 and annexed in 1908.

Slovenia, wedged between Austria, Italy, and Croatia at the foot of the Alps, was another Catholic area, but with its own unique language. Most of the other nationalities spoke a version of Serbo-Croat, even if the alphabets they used varied. Slovenia was part of the Austro-Hungarian Empire, but it also experienced a surge in nationalist sentiment, particularly after the continent-wide revolutions of 1848.[2]

Macedonians lived in the region bordering today's Greece, which was still part of the Ottoman Empire in the early 19th century, and Macedonia also bordered Albania and Bulgaria. Macedonia had particular links with the latter, including linguistically and culturally, and the territory included a significant minority of ethnic Albanians. Macedonia proved to have one of the most potent national movements of the era, manifesting itself notoriously as the Macedonian Revolutionary Organization (MRO), which, although relatively small in number, played a role in weakening the Ottoman Empire.

Montenegrins were the last piece of the ethnic jigsaw puzzle. Set on the Adriatic Sea, Montenegro had come under the control of the Ottomans, Habsburgs, and Venetians at various times. The tiny country gained principality status in 1852 and then full independence from the Ottomans in 1878. Traditionally, Montenegro had been close to Serbia and fought on the same side during the First World War, but it was occupied by Austrian forces between 1916-1918.

As the Austro-Hungarian and Ottoman Empires teetered in the late 19th century, Balkan countries all sought to expand their borders.[3] In their own ways, each Balkan nation had what was known as a "Big Idea" (from the Greek "Megali Idea"), a project to maximize its boundaries to the furthest possible point and incorporate various historical claims. The list of conflicts is long and perplexing, and it included the war between the Russians and the Ottomans that culminated in the 1878 Congress of Berlin, presided over by German Chancellor Otto von Bismarck. The year 1878 saw an increase in Serbia's territory, independence for other countries from the Ottomans, and the Austrian occupation of Bosnia and Herzegovina. The Treaty of San Stefano confirmed the territorial changes, in particular the enlargement of Bulgaria.

From the Congress of Berlin until 1914, Balkan countries would be locked into competition, making the region a cauldron of violence and instability.[4] In addition, the Great Powers felt compelled to involve themselves in the region. It appeared that Russia backed change and the dismemberment of the Ottoman Empire, whereas Britain seemed to support the status quo encapsulated by the existing situation.[5]

[2] Oto Luthar, *The Land Between: A History of Slovenia* (Frankfurt am Main: Peter Lang, 2008), p. 280.
[3] Mark Mazower, *The Balkans: From the End of Byzantium to the Present Day* (London: Phoenix, 2001), p. 126.
[4] Misha Glenny, *The Balkans 1804-2012: Nationalism, War and the Great Powers* (London: Granta, 2012), pp. 133-134.
[5] Tom Gallagher, *Outcast Europe: The Balkans, 1789-1989: From the Ottomans to Milošević,* (London: Routledge,

Along with the conflicts between empires and states, a number of events and movements within the Balkan countries themselves would affect the foundation of Yugoslavia. In June 1903, a group of Serb army plotters, led by Captain Dragutin Dimitrijević (otherwise known as Aspis), assassinated the pro-Austrian Serb King Alexander Obrenović and his wife in Belgrade, as well the Prime Minister.[6] The crown then passed to the Karađorđević family and King Pete I. The new monarch gave a free hand over government policy to the military while being more sympathetic to Russia. As a result, Serb policy developed in a more hostile fashion towards the Austro-Hungarian Empire.[7] Intrigue in Serbia, however, was not over. Aspis later founded the secret Black Hand organisation of Serb nationalists in 1911. The Black Hand would gain historical infamy with its role in starting the First World War and Gavrilo Princip was its notorious member. Macedonian underground groups were also active during the first years of the 20th century and launched an uprising in 1903, put down by 40,000 Ottoman troops.

2001), p. 31.
[6] Richard J. Evans, The Pursuit of Power: Europe 1815-1914 (London: Penguin, 2017), p. 691.
[7] Ibid, p. 691.

Драгутин Т. Димитријевић-Апис

Dragutin Dimitrijević

Aleksandar

Meanwhile, in the Ottoman Empire, a group of disgruntled military units and underground organisations, revolted in 1908. Known as the "Young Turk Revolution," the uprising was the beginning of the end of the empire and the rise of Turkish nationalism. To its neighbors, the Young Turk revolt was proof that the Ottomans were in weakened position, and Austria's response was to formally annex Bosnia and Herzegovina.[8] It would not be long before others attempted to fill the power vacuum.

The uncertainty in the Balkan region provided impetus for all the nationalist groups as the

---

[8] Misha Glenny, *The Balkans 1804-2012: Nationalism, War and the Great Powers* (London: Granta, 2012), pp. 218-219.

empires went into terminal decline, and the situation erupted in a number of conflicts in 1912 and 1913 that became known as the Balkan Wars. Albanian tribesmen occupied Skopje (the capital of today's Republic of Macedonia), providing the spark for others to move. In October 1912, Bulgaria, Greece, Montenegro, and Serbia all commenced hostilities, attempting to expand their territory.[9] Soon it was the Serbs that occupied Skopje. Meanwhile, Greek forces occupied the ancient port city of Salonika, pushing out the Ottomans after hundreds of years.

The fighting threatened to drag in the larger powers, and consequently the British convened a peace conference. The Treaty of London was signed in May 1913 to draw the map of the region, essentially without the Ottomans.[10] Soon afterwards, however, fighting resumed and Bulgaria gained land, confirmed in the Treaties of Bucharest and Constantinople.[11]

The wars had been relatively short in duration, but the modern military techniques had proven destructive, killing 200,000 men on all sides. As historian Richard J. Evans noted, "These wars were a portent of things to come."[12] The Balkan Wars also created a certain picture of the region in the minds of Western Europeans, especially as reports from the period described Balkan "barbarism" and particularism in the savagery undertaken by combatants.[13] It was a reputation that lasted the entire 20th century, and it was so powerful that outside powers tried to justify intervention in the Balkan conflicts of 1912-1913 through Christian "Just War Thinking," invoking a duty to prevent savagery.[14]

World War I in the Balkans

Following the 1903 coup that installed Karađorđević on the Serbian throne, the country had internalized an anti-Austrian foreign policy. One of the offshoots of this stance was the Black Hand organisation, set up by the 1903 conspirators. It has been assumed that the plot to assassinate the Austro-Hungarian heir to the Imperial Crown, Archduke Franz Ferdinand, was supported by the Serbian government, but the truth was probably more complex. The Black Hand was a nationalist Serb outfit with links to the country's military and the goal of expanding the boundaries of Serbia to include all ethnic Serbs. This would include ethnic Serbs who lived in other parts of the Balkans, including Bosnia-Herzegovina.

Gavrilo Princip himself was born in Bosnia, and though he later claimed to be a Yugoslav nationalist wanting to free the Slavic people from Austrian domination, it was no coincidence that Princip and his group of collaborators chose June 28, 1914 to assassinate Franz Ferdinand. That date was the anniversary of the Serbs' iconic battle, the 1389 Battle of Kosovo. The desire

[9] Richard J. Evans, The Pursuit of Power: Europe 1815-1914 (London: Penguin, 2017), p. 693.
[10] Ibid, p. 695.
[11] Ibid, p. 695.
[12] Ibid, p. 697.
[13] Eugene Michail, 'Western Attitudes to War in the Balkans and the Shifting Meanings of Violence, 1912-1991', Journal of Contemporary History, (47:219, 2012), pp. 219-241)), p. 220.
[14] Ibid, p. 222.

to maximize Serbia's land - essentially the Serbs' "Big Idea" - would come back to haunt the Yugoslav project at the end of the 20th century.

The world reacted with horror to the assassination of Franz Ferdinand and his wife Sophie, nowhere more so than throughout Austria-Hungary, where there was widespread rioting against innocent Serbian citizens living within the empire's borders. It is surmized that many of those displaced eventually made their way back across the border to Serbia as refugees, further inflaming sentiment against Austrians and making an already volatile situation that much worse. Expressions of horror and commiseration came in from Germany, France, Britain (although the public and the government's attention there were far more focused on the rapidly escalating crisis in Ireland, where the independence movement had turned violent), and even Austria's recent enemy, Italy. Russia also offered its condolences, which was quite hypocritical given that the Russian government was almost certainly aware of the Serbian plot.

Overwhelmingly, the Great Powers sided with Austria, and a joint Austro-Hungarian and German demand was presented to the Serbian government to commence an internal investigation into the assassination, but the Serbian Ministry of Foreign Affairs dismissed such a request out of hand, claiming that there was absolutely nothing to investigate. This further aggravated an already awkward situation.

In the wake of the investigation into the death of Franz Ferdinand and the resulting trial and sentences that followed, along with the verdict of the court inculpating Serbia for the murders, the Austro-Hungarian Empire ultimately issued a letter to Serbia which became known as the July Ultimatum. This inflammatory letter demanded that the Kingdom of Serbia repudiate in writing the acts of the terrorists intent on destabilizing the legitimacy of the Austro-Hungarian monarchy and their hold over Bosnia-Herzegovina, and it also reminded the Serbian government that it had bound itself to abide by the terms of the agreement ceding it to Austria-Hungary in the first place. The letter also listed 10 key points which Serbia was expected to accept within 48 hours, and it threatened retaliation in the case of non-compliance.

The points listed were as follows:

1.   Serbia must renounce all propaganda designed to inspire hatred towards Austria-Hungary and which might prove harmful to its territorial integrity.

2.   The Organization known as the People's Defence must be disbanded forthwith, along with all organizations of a similar ilk.

3.   All propaganda against Austria-Hungary published in public documents, including school textbooks, is to be eliminated forthwith.

4.   All officers and government officials named by the Austro-Hungarian government are to be removed from office immediately.

5.   Members of the Austro-Hungarian government will be dispatched immediately to Belgrade, where they are to be given every assistance in suppressing subversive movements.

6.   All those involved in Franz Ferdinand's assassination are to be brought to trial forthwith, with the assistance of police investigators from Austria-Hungary.

7.   Major Vojislav Tankosic and Milan Ciganovic, known participants in the assassination of the royal couple, are to be immediately arrested.

8.   The Serbian government must cease all collusion in the transportation of weapons and equipment across the Austro-Hungarian Border, dismissing and disciplining the Border Patrol officials at Sabac and Loznica, who abetted the Sarajevo conspirators.

9.   Provide suitable explanation to the Austro-Hungarian government with regards to the actions undertaken by certain Serbian officials, who have demonstrated an attitude of hostility in their negotiations with the Austrian government.

10.   Immediately notify the Austro-Hungarian government once these measures have been enacted.

The letter set off a frantic flurry of activity in Serbia, but not of the kind the Austro-Hungarians wanted, aside from those in office who were clearly spoiling for a fight. Serbia telegraphed to St Petersburg asking for support, which Russia promised in the event of a fight. Reassured, Serbia then mobilized its armed forces before sending a reply to the July Ultimatum that conceded both points 8 and 10 but rejected the remaining points. The Serbs disguized their explicit refusal with a wealth of diplomatic actions that did nothing to fool the Austro-Hungarian government. The response from the empire was swift; the Austro-Hungarian ambassador in Belgrade was recalled, and troops began to prepare in for mobilization.

A propaganda cartoon after the assassination that asserted "Serbia must die!"

The day after the Austro-Hungarian ambassador departed from Belgrade, a convoy of Serbian troops being transported down the Danube River by steamer drifted off course towards the Austro-Hungarian bank near Temes-Kubin, where the local garrison commander ordered shots fired into the air to discourage them from landing. He wisely avoided firing upon the boats, which might well have precipitated a full-scale crisis, but as it was, his level-headedness would be to no avail. Unfortunately, the report which reached Emperor Franz Joseph I in Vienna about this incident inaccurately portrayed the trifling affair as a bloody last-ditch skirmish, and Franz Joseph I responded by declaring war. The Austrian Army was brought forward to a state of full mobilization, and the allotted divisions moved forward to their position on the Serbian border.

This was the move that set the dominoes of war in motion. Russia and France immediately mobilized their armies in response to the Austro-Hungarian threat, as they were required to do so according to the terms of the Secret Treaty of 1892, which stated that any mobilization of members of the Triple Alliance must be met. The initial, limited mobilization by Austria-Hungary was followed by a full-scale Russian one, which in turn was followed by a full-scale German and Austro-Hungarian call-up, which in turn precipitated a French one and finally a British one. Thus, with a suddenness that startled even those who felt it was inevitable, the major European powers all found themselves at war.

Although there had been explicit displays of commiseration and sympathy for Austria and widespread condemnation of Serbia's actions in the immediate aftermath of Franz Ferdinand's assassination, the attitude of the great powers towards Austria as the notional aggrieved party became substantially chillier as Austria insisted on virtually bullying Serbia over the whole affair. The British Prime Minister, Asquith, complained in an official letter that Serbia had no hope of appeasing Austria diplomatically, and that the terms of the July Ultimatum would've been impossible to meet even if Serbia was willing to do so. Indeed, it appears as though such an exacting document had been drafted precisely because Serbia didn't have a hope of complying, even if they had so wished, and thus Austria-Hungary would be able to go to war and punish them properly for the outrage perpetrated against their royal family.

100 years removed from the assassination, it might be unfair to say that it caused World War I, but it certainly started it. Historians still debate whether the Great War would have occurred even if Franz Ferdinand and Sophie lived out their lives in peace and comfort, but many believe that while it might've come months or years down the road, it was inevitable. The tangled web of alliances at cross-purposes, the growing diplomatic tensions, the arms race, the belligerence of newly powerful states such as Germany, the interference in other sovereign countries' affairs, and the relentless politicking all pointed towards one tragic outcome.

As for the parties themselves, it's apparent that much of the blame can be shouldered by the Serbian government. To this day, it's still unclear how much the King and Prime Minister knew about the plots and actions carried out by Dimitrijević and his associates in the Black Hand, but they were obviously privy to the official communications that involved Dimitrijević in his capacity as the head of Serbian Military Intelligence. Furthermore, it was the Serbian government, not the Black Hand (which at that point was virtually synonymous with Dimitrijević and Military Intelligence in any case) that provided Princip, Grabež, Cubrilovic, and the other conspirators with their firearms, explosives, training, and the means to cross the border into Bosnia. The People's Defence, the clandestine group within Bosnia, had been almost completely taken over by Serbian Military Intelligence and was effectively acting as a shell organization. Government officials from several different agencies had colluded with the conspirators on many occasions, with the end result that on the day of the assassination, the assassins were in place, suitably organized, well-armed for their purpose, and ready for action. At the same time, there are strong indications that several officials within the Serbian government (with or without sanction from on high) attempted to warn their Austro-Hungarian counterparts of what was to come.

Another country that must bear a share of the blame is Russia. According to the confession given by Dimitrijević at the end of his 1917 trial in Salonika, Russia was fully aware of his activities, and he had no reason to lie at that point. Indeed, according to Dimitrijević, the Russian Military Attachè in Belgrade had guaranteed that Russia would stand with Serbia against Austria-Hungary in the event that the operation was compromised, and that he had received funds from Russia to carry out the assassination. An investigative journalist attempting to uncover the truth received a fairly unconvincing testimony from the Russian Military Attachè, who denied any involvement. The Russian Military Attachè claimed that his Assistant had been in charge during the period leading up to the assassination, and that Dimitrijević never apprized him of his plans or intentions. It has also been suggested that the Tsar, or at the very least the Prime Minister, were aware of a forthcoming attempt against Franz Ferdinand's life and were not opposed to it happening. Russia had a vested interest both in weakening the Austro-Hungarian Empire and in destabilizing its hold on the Balkans as this might well potentially give it access to the strategically invaluable Mediterranean ports without having to pass through the Turkish-controlled Bosphorus and Dardanelles straits, which hampered its attempts to increase its naval power outside of the Black Sea.

Even Austria-Hungary, despite being the aggrieved party, had a hand in what followed the assassination. The Austro-Hungarian military had resisted many attempts at pacification with Serbia, including policies advocated by Franz Ferdinand himself, and it continued to pursue a policy of aggressive saber-rattling. Furthermore, the Governor of Bosnia, Oskar Potiorek, was a rigid and stubborn individual who viewed Slavic patriots as a national security threat and ruthlessly punished them accordingly, further inflaming anti-Austrian sentiment in a newly created province that required the most delicate of management rather than hamfisted pacification attempts. His refusal to countenance the use of improperly dressed troops to shield Franz Ferdinand and his halting of the motorcade in a vulnerable position near the bank of the river were symptomatic of his stubbornness, and his decision to remain idle while Sarajevo tore apart the homes of hundreds of innocent Serbs is evidence of his poor character.

Ironically, one of the few people who had no blame in what was to come was Franz Ferdinand himself. A choleric individual with the typical Austrian aristocrat's condescending attitude towards the subordinate Hungarian population, he was nonetheless no more prejudiced than many during his time and a great deal less than most; after all, he married a woman from the Czech aristocracy who was beneath his station. On top of that, his attitude towards Serbia and the Slavic issue was remarkably conciliatory for someone in his position. He went to his death unwittingly even after bravely continuing his public appearance despite having a hand grenade hurled at him. It is unfortunate for Franz Ferdinand that his birth and position made him an ideal target, but as history and fate would have it, he was simply the right man in the wrong place at the wrong time.

World War I engulfed many parts of the world, and it is mostly remembered due to the trench warfare on the Western Front, but the Balkans experienced the war very differently. It was a more fluid war, and it fundamentally changed every aspect of life in the region. In some cases, fighting in the Balkans dragged on into the 1920s, while the populations were "exchanged" on the basis of nationality.

The future Yugoslav Republics were pitted against each other from 1914-1918. The Ottomans aligned with Germany and Austria, which included Croatia, Slovenia, and Bosnia and Herzegovina.[15] Serbia fought against the Central Powers along with Montenegro. Somewhat ironically, it would be Serbia that came out of the conflict in the strongest position.

The war would decimate the Austro-Hungarian and Ottoman Empires, but their armies were still significantly larger than any of the smaller Balkan states that formed Yugoslavia. Serbia fought stoutly against the Austrians, but attacks from both the north and the east forced the Serb army to retreat in 1915. Its soldiers went on a long march through Kosovo and Albania before taking refuge in Greece.[16] Serbian King Peter I formed a government-in-exile on the island of Corfu, while the Macedonian and Montenegrin forces joined the Serbs in retreat.

King Peter I

When Russia transformed as a result of the revolution in 1917 and sought an armistice shortly afterwards, it appeared that Serbia had lost its vital benefactor, but the war ended the following year with British, Italian, and French troops finally defeating the Germans, Austro-Hungarians, and Ottomans. Those Balkan countries that had aligned themselves with the Allied forces would certainly benefit when the post-war geopolitical compact was settled at Versailles.

With the old empires in tatters by the end of the war, and with Russia incapacitated by its revolution, British and French power now dominated in the Balkans. Both had huge overseas empires of their own and were keen to expand their influence in the wider region, from the Balkans to the Middle East and North Africa.

Crucially for the story of Yugoslavia, Britain and France both favored Serbia.[17] Some writers

---

[15] David Owen, *Balkan Odyssey* (London: Indigo, 1996), p. 7.
[16] Ibid, p. 7.
[17] Eugene Michail, 'Western Attitudes to War in the Balkans and the Shifting Meanings of Violence, 1912-1991',

have put this in the context of the romantic nationalists that came to prominence in the 19th century, based first on liberating the Greeks (*Philhellenism*) from the Ottoman Empire and then other Christian national movements in the region. Indeed, London was home to a number of exiled nationalist movements. The more likely reason for the British and French support was that the Serbs made up the largest contingent in the West Balkan area. Therefore, support for Serbia may have offered the larger powers their best hope of stability, and this morphed into support for a Serb-led Slavic state.

The Formation of Yugoslavia

There were very few people within the Balkans who backed a Yugoslav state before 1918.[18] The concept of a union of the different nationalities in the region was the brainchild of a limited group of thinkers, which ensured Yugoslavia was essentially a top-down project. The two key architects of the state were Nikola Pašić, a Serb, and Ante Trumbić, a Croat.[19] The pair set up the "Yugoslav National Committee" in Paris in 1915, and this culminated in the July 1917 "Corfu Declaration," which set out the basis of a Yugoslav state, or a Kingdom of Serbs, Croats and Slovenes as it was then known.[20] France and Britain became early supporters of the Yugoslav project, seeing it as a potential bulwark against previous foes. Some, but by no means all British and French policy-makers believed that a Southern Slav state could prevent further instability in the region, which had been so instrumental in causing the war in the first place.

Journal of Contemporary History, (47:219, 2012), pp. 219-241)), p. 220.

[18] Mark Mazower, *The Balkans: From the End of Byzantium to the Present Day* (London: Phoenix, 2001), p. 114.

[19] Robert Gerwarth, *The Vanquished: Why the First World War Failed to End, 1917-1923* (London: Allen Lane, 2016), p. 189.

[20] Ibid, p. 197.

Pašić

Nikola Pašić was already in his late 60s by the start of World War I and had a long career in Serbian politics behind him. Pašić was Prime Minister in 1914 when the Austrians presented him with the "July Ultimatum," and although he accepted most of its demands, Vienna concluded that the Serb government and the "Black Hand" were one and the same. In exile during the war, Pašić became the leading Serb negotiator for the idea of a unified Slav state. During his long career, Pašić was most adept at gaining and accumulating power. Coupled with the instincts of Serb nationalism, he may have seen the Yugoslav project as a means of extending its influence.[21]

Although he may not have been personally enthusiastic about the idea, he was faithful to the wishes of the Serbian regent, Alexander, who was. Pašić also believed a number of assurances

[21] Misha Glenny, *The Balkans 1804-2012: Nationalism, War and the Great Powers* (London: Granta, 2012), p. 369.

had been made to the Croats and Slovenes during the war, alluding to a security alliance that needed to be honored in forming a unified state.

Croat leader Ante Trumbić, born in 1864, may have been even more fervent in desiring a unified nation. During the war, Croatia was forced to fight with the Austrians, but Trumbić, leading the London-based Yugoslav National Committee, lobbied the Allied Powers to accept the idea of Yugoslavia after the end of the conflict.[22] On July 20, 1917, the Corfu Declaration was signed and laid the foundation for Trumbić and Pašić's state. Shortly after the end of the First World War, on December 1, 1918, a Kingdom of Serbs, Croats and Slovenes was declared. Several days earlier, Serbia had formed a separate union with its ally Montenegro.[23] The Great Powers left the final settling of the state's borders for the imminent Versailles Conference, to be held near Paris.

Trumbić

Even before the state's foundation, tensions began to simmer between the different

---

[22] David Owen, *Balkan Odyssey* (London: Indigo, 1996), p. 7.
[23] Dejan Djokic, 'Versailles and Yugoslavia: ninety years on', *Open Democracy*, 26 June 2009, https://www.opendemocracy.net/article/versailles-and-yugoslavia-ninety-years-on

nationalities. The Croats and Slovenes saw the benefits of a united Slav state in terms of security; having been occupied for centuries by the Austrians, they were now wary of an expansionist Italy, which, having been on the side of the victors during the First World War, now sought territorial recompense. In particular, the Italians were making a claim on parts of the Dalmatian Coast in Croatia. The pooling of resources could buttress Croatia and Slovenia against outside threats, and ultimately this was crucial in the acceptance of a unified state under Serbian leadership.[24]

Nevertheless, a key principle was left unresolved between Pašić and Trumbić that would repeatedly come back to haunt Yugoslavia. Trumbić and the Croats believed they were signing up for a loose federation in which the component republics, namely Croatia, would have significant autonomy. Pašić and the Serbs, however, favored a unitary and more centralized state, naturally led by the majority Serbs. This tension led to several constitutions, a number of revolts, and the collapse of the country altogether generations later.[25]

In modern history books, the Treaty of Versailles looms large. Ostensibly called to formalize the end of the war, the prominent decision-makers at Versailles sought to punish the aggressors in the war and to stabilize Europe, in order to prevent further conflagration. The conference has been interpreted in many ways, but it is most widely remembered today as punishing Germany so harshly that it inadvertently led to World War II.

Versailles also brought about the creation of a number of new states, including Yugoslavia. The three major players at Versailles were French Prime Minister Georges Clemenceau, British Prime Minister David Lloyd George, and American President Woodrow Wilson. President Wilson came to Versailles with a separate, although clearly related set of priorities. Having issued his famous "Fourteen Points" for ending the war in January 1918, Wilson put more emphasis on democratic accountability and self-determination. At Versailles, this meant that new states were formed while border territories were given the option, through plebiscites, of choosing whether to join one state or another.[26]

This also meant that numerous delegations arrived at Versailles putting forward their cases for national sovereignty. For Yugoslavia, Nikola Pašić and Ante Trumbić were there, as well as nationalists from the countries that would constitute the unified state. These included an obscure Croatian nationalist by the name of Ante Pavelić, who was opposed to the Yugoslav idea, believing it to be a "Greater Serbia" project.[27] Pavelić would become one of the most notorious

---

[24] Mark Mazower, *The Balkans: From the End of Byzantium to the Present Day* (London: Phoenix, 2001), p. 114, David Owen, *Balkan Odyssey* (London: Indigo, 1996), p. 7.

[25] Robert Gerwarth, *The Vanquished: Why the First World War Failed to End, 1917-1923* (London: Allen Lane, 2016), p. 198.

[26] Godfrey Hodgson, *People's Century: From the dawn of the century to the eve of the millennium* (Godalming: BBC Books, 1998), p. 80.

[27] Robert Gerwarth, *The Vanquished: Why the First World War Failed to End, 1917-1923* (London: Allen Lane, 2016), p. 189.

figures in the state's history.

Pavelić

One of the key problems for the architects of the post-war world in Versailles was that when Wilson's ideas came into contact with reality, sovereignty and self-determination for some was not inclusive for others. It would prove impossible to draw borders containing discreet national groups, and this was evident within the multinational Kingdom of Serbs, Croats and Slovenes. Despite the liberal, progressive rhetoric at Versailles, the new states clearly included minorities that either did not want to live in the new arrangement or would be persecuted by the majority group.

Czechoslovakia and the Kingdom of Serbs, Croats and Slovenes were among the new states that officially came into being on June 28, 1919, five years after Gavrilo Princip had assassinated

Franz Ferdinand in Sarajevo. In Yugoslavia's case, a better way of describing Versailles was that its creation was not opposed by the Great Powers.[28] Moreover, the young state still had border disputes with Italy and Romania which remained unsettled until the 1920s.[29]

As the dust settled after Versailles, the Yugoslav delegation returned home to start the serious business of building a new state from scratch. Due to its previous domination by different empires, not to mention its different languages, cultures, and traditions, the separate republics had quite different structures. Pašić was temporarily out of power in the new state, while Trumbić was appointed foreign minister. Serbian monarch King Peter I assumed power over the new country, while his son, Alexander, wielded influence behind the scenes as Regent.

Alexander I

The early formation of Yugoslavia was quite different from the federal version that emerged

[28] Dejan Djokic, 'Versailles and Yugoslavia: ninety years on', *Open Democracy*, 26 June 2009,
https://www.opendemocracy.net/article/versailles-and-yugoslavia-ninety-years-on
[29] Ibid.

after 1945. It contained six customs areas, five currencies, four rail networks, three banking systems, and initially two seats of government in Belgrade and Zagreb.[30] The region was overwhelmingly an agricultural economy, as approximately 75% of the population still worked on the land.[31] The state was split into a number of provinces, which broadly speaking can be seen as Slovenia, Croatia, Serbia, Bosnia, and Montenegro.

The new state, despite being a multiethnic formulation, paid little attention to a number of other nationalities present in the region in 1918. These included ethnic Germans, Greeks, Turks, Hungarians, Romanians, and Albanians.[32] Although the politics of the Kingdom bore some semblance to its European contemporaries - for instance a Social Democratic party existed, as well as the Democratic Party - there were numerous ethnically based parties, such as the Serbian Radicals, the Croatian Peasant Party, and the Slovenian People's Party. The Croat Peasants, dominated by Stjepan Radić, were initially proponents of an agrarian socialism and Croat autonomy, while the Democrats were the major voices for a centralized state.

Radić

[30] David Owen, *Balkan Odyssey* (London: Indigo, 1996), p. 7.
[31] Misha Glenny, *The Balkans 1804-2012: Nationalism, War and the Great Powers* (London: Granta, 2012), p. 396.
[32] David Owen, *Balkan Odyssey* (London: Indigo, 1996), p. 7.

Immediate Instability

One of the first challenges for the new state was to pass a constitution. The document barely achieved parliamentary consent on June 28, 1921 after having been proposed the previous year. In fact, it achieved only a simple majority, as opposed to the 60% stipulated in the Corfu Declaration.[33] It became known as the "Vidovdan Constitution," as it shared the date of the famous remembrance of Serb national identity.

A new administrative structure was set out in the document, with 33 new Oblasts (provinces) essentially forming a unitary, Serb-led, centralized monarchy. Nationalists in the smaller non-Serb areas were outraged. For Croats and Slovenes, this was a betrayal of the agreements made during the First World War. Support for the new state weakened in its peripheral regions throughout the next two decades, and almost immediately, peasant groups violently opposed the 1921 constitution.[34] Indeed, the battle over the constitution paralyzed politics over the first half of the 1920s, with the main Croat nationalist leaders refusing to participate.

The dominant figures in the first phase of Yugoslavia were politicians such as Nikola Pašić and the Karađorđević monarchy. The Karađorđević family had been locked in a battle for influence in Serbia throughout the 19th century with the Obrenović family. The former was pro-Russian, while the latter was pro-Austrian, and each wanted to reduce the influence of the opposing power.

The 1903 coup that murdered the Obrenović king appeared to have settled the Serbian monarchy question, and King Peter I had been on the throne as Serbia gone through the successes and failures of World War I and the formation of the Kingdom of Serbs, Croats and Slovenes. Peter I now projected more Serb influence than had existed, in the Serbian nationalists' eyes, for hundreds of years.

It was Peter I's son, Alexander, however, who was the more committed supporter of a unified Yugoslav state of Southern Slavs. Alexander, then 32 years old, became king in August 1921 following the death of his father, and he would play a pivotal role in the historical development of Yugoslavia over the next decade. King Alexander I's erratic rule proved antagonistic to the ethnic minorities within the state, particularly the Croats, and this rivalry overshadowed the early years of the country. Croat nationalists were not the only minority to sour over the idea of Yugoslavia, as some of the most potent challenges to the new state were Macedonian underground groups.

The IMRO (Internal Macedonian Revolutionary Organization, the successor of the MRO) had already made its mark on Balkan history thanks to its campaign of improvized violence and subversion at the turn of the century. In a unified Yugoslavia, the Macedonians were clearly

[33] Misha Glenny, *The Balkans 1804-2012: Nationalism, War and the Great Powers* (London: Granta, 2012), p. 403.
[34] Mark Mazower, *The Balkans: From the End of Byzantium to the Present Day* (London: Phoenix, 2001), p. 114.

subjugated behind other nationalities, and the IMRO and other Macedonia underground groups such as the Macedonian Federative Organization (MFO) renewed their provocative activities. During the 1920s, the IMRO circulated rumours that Italy was about to invade, causing grave concern among Croats in particular.[35] The IMRO had a number of objectives, ranging from gaining separate autonomy within a Balkan Federation to being incorporated into the Bulgarian state.

The Kingdom of Serbs, Croats and Slovenes ostensibly managed to settle its boundary questions with the Treaty of Rapallo in November 1920. Located south of Genoa, the Rapallo document was signed by the Yugoslavs and Italy, settling the status of Dalmatia and Istria within Croatia. For the Croats, however, this was a bitter pill to swallow, as the Treaty proposed independent sovereignty over a number of cities in Istria and Dalmatia, including Rijeka (known as Fiume to Italians).[36] Nikola Pašić had disturbed the Croats in the Yugoslav delegation during the wartime negotiations with the Allied Powers through his potential willingness to sign over Croat and Slovene land to the Italians in return for land favored by Serb nationalists in Macedonia and Albania.[37] Indeed, as Prime Minister, Nikola Pašić formally signed these territories over to Benito Mussolini in January 1924, much to the dismay of Croats. Meanwhile the newly formed countries in the region – Yugoslavia, Czechoslovakia and Romania – formed the so-called "Little Entente," an alliance to improve their respective positions against the former imperial powers, in 1920.

Pašić had returned to office in 1921 and became the dominant figure in the first years of the nation. Although Yugoslavia was nominally democratic, these institutions never took root in the first decades of the state's existence.[38] Much was made of this in later years, but clearly democracy in the Balkans was relatively novel. Moreover, if voters simply supported parties of their own nationality, democracy was likely to be extremely difficult. The only idea that truly cut across the different ethnicities was socialism, and this would not gain broad support for awhile. In the 1920s, political parties found it difficult to appeal to several part of the nation.

Croat separatists such as Radić came in behind the Belgrade authorities for a time in the mid-1920s. The Croatian leader had been jailed in January 1925 on charges that his party had broken a 1920 law, the Obznana Decree, which had been initially designed to suppress the Communist Party. Shortly afterwards, however, Radić stunned his opponents and supporters alike by throwing his weight behind the Vidovdan Constitution. In fact, the Croatian Peasant Party leader came to an agreement with King Alexander I due to the threat posed to Croatian integrity by Mussolini's fascist Italy. The king realized he needed his country's two biggest parties to come to terms with each other if he was to achieve stability. Therefore, Radić instructed his nephew to

[35] Nada Boskovska, *Yugoslavia and Macedonia Before Tito: Between Repression and Integration* (London: IB Tauris, 2016)

[36] Misha Glenny, *The Balkans 1804-2012: Nationalism, War and the Great Powers* (London: Granta, 2012), p. 377.

[37] Ibid, pp. 369, 377.

[38] David Owen, *Balkan Odyssey* (London: Indigo, 1996), p. 7.

make a statement to the Belgrade parliament: "The Vidovdan Constitution exists here today de facto, this is a political fact of life, with the Karadjordjević (Karađorđević) dynasty as the head of the state. This is a fact which we accept unconditionally and with which we agree…Although it may look as though we have made concessions to our brothers, those brothers are the Serbian people and represent our joint future together."[39]

Radić was released from prison shortly after the declaration, and the development was a major breakthrough in the already fractious history of Yugoslavia. King Alexander I brokered a coalition agreement between the Serbian Radicals and Radić's Croatian Peasant Party, and for a time the country seemed to be moving into a new phase of peace and prosperity. The economies of major cities such as Zagreb and Belgrade appeared to boom.

The truce only lasted, however, until the next round of discord threatened to overwhelm the fragile state. Pašić resigned in 1926 due to a corruption scandal, and his son Rade was implicated in a number of graft allegations that became a point of constant criticism from the Croatian Peasant Party.[40]

Relations between the Serb Radicals and Croatian Peasant Party deteriorated after Pašić, a flawed politician but one who could at least claim to represent some continuity, resigned. The parliament, known as the Skupština, became home to almost daily shouting matches, intimidations, and squabbles which threatened to turn violent. Stjepan Radić himself had been threatened on several occasions by other parliamentarians.

On June 19, 1928, a member of the Serb Radicals, Puniša Račić, pulled out a revolver in the parliament and shot three Croatian Peasant Party MPs, including Radić. The Croat leader initially appeared to recover, but he died on August 8 of that year.[41] The assassinations caused outrage across the country, especially in Croatia. The government attempted to struggle on, but disputes only grew, and coalitions proved impossible to form.

On January 6, 1929, King Alexander I suspended the democracy and effectively seized power for himself as part of a monarchical dictatorship. Alexander renamed the Kingdom of Serbs, Croats and Slovenes in October 1929 to the more familiar Yugoslavia, loosely translated as Land of the Southern Slavs.

The king remained obsessed with the "Croat Question," and how to pacify the demands of Croat separatists while maintaining the integrity of the Yugoslav project. It is worth noting that the other nationalities did not always support Croat claims of Serb dominance. Indeed, the Slovene People's Party and the (Bosnian) Yugoslav Muslim Organization often supported Belgrade in the disputes with Zagreb in the 1920s.[42]

[39] Misha Glenny, *The Balkans 1804-2012: Nationalism, War and the Great Powers* (London: Granta, 2012), p. 405.
[40] Ibid, p. 407.
[41] Ibid, pp. 408-412.

Nonetheless, Croat nationalists were certainly developing greater animus to the Yugoslav state by the end of the decade. The controversy over the Vidovdan Constitution, territorial concessions to Italy, and the 1928 assassinations had provided much fuel to the separatist fire. The feeling held by Croat nationalists was that Yugoslavia was a Greater Serbian project that was either indifferent, or at worst hostile to Croat sentiments. Radić's funeral – acting as a locus of Croatian nationalism and grievance - was attended by hundreds of thousands, and the red and white chequered flag, subsequently synonymous with the Ustaše terrorist group, was brandished at the funeral for the first time.

Another Croat nationalist, Ante Pavelić, fled Yugoslavia in 1929, having contacted the IMRO. Pavelić had already established an underground Croat group, known as the Ustaše, from the acronym UHRO (Croatian Revolutionary Organisation). The Ustaše attracted emigres who were living in exile across Europe, particularly Austria, and started a campaign of violence and assassinations within Yugoslavia. Pavelić was tried and sentenced to death in Yugoslavia, but by this point he had fled into exile in Mussolini's Italy.[43] This suited Mussolini, who had come to power in 1922 and saw the possibility of splitting Yugoslavia and gaining greater regional influence for Italy.

Many more Yugoslavs would become sympathetic to groups such as the Ustaše and the IMRO after October 1929 and the Wall Street Crash. Although the crash took place in the United States, it impacted virtually every economy that participated in the global trading system. King Alexander I responded to the crisis in a number of ways, strengthening central (that is to say Serb) control over the economy. The national minorities in Yugoslavia believed that they suffered more economic pain than the majority Serbs, therefore intensifying the rivalries and animosities that had built up in the 1920s. The country was straining under the limits of the Gold Standard, and the level of its foreign trade declined.

King Alexander I had also reorganized the administrative structure of his country shortly after its name change to Yugoslavia. 33 Oblasts became nine new regions, or *banovinas*, and in 1931 he signed a new constitution that put executive power officially in the hands of the monarch. Democracy in Yugoslavia had been officially extinguished.

Alexander formed a separate autocratic tool for his decrees, called the "Court for the Protection of the State," which stifled any opposition to the king. The Court quickly arrested the two most prominent opposition politicians, Vladko Maček and Svetozar Pribićević. Maček had become leader of the Croatian Peasant Party after Stjepan Radić's assassination in 1928, and as a leading opponent of the king, he was jailed in 1933 for treason. Svetozar Pribićević, on the other hand, was a Serb from Croatia who strongly supported the idea of Yugoslavia. Pribićević had been a Democrat before setting up a splinter party, but, having changed his mind about a centralizing

---

[42] Misha Glenny, *The Balkans 1804-2012: Nationalism, War and the Great Powers* (London: Granta, 2012), p. 408.
[43] Ibid, p. 430.

approach, formed a political partnership with Croat nationalists such as Radić. He was jailed in 1929 but released in 1931 due to poor health. Pribićević became a leading critic of Alexander's dictatorship from exile in Paris before his death in 1936.

Extrajudicial killings were also prevalent. In February 1931, a leading Croatian intellectual who opposed Yugoslavia, Milan Šufflay, was murdered outside his home by members of the royalist Young Yugoslavia group. The murder provoked an international outcry.

Ante Pavelić, in exile in Italy, took more extreme positions during the 1930s.[44] His vision for an independent Croat state incorporated more and more of Yugoslavia. Pavelić was developing his own "Big Idea" of Croatia, as many Croats lived in Bosnia and Herzegovina as well as regions of Serbia. The Ustaše leader appealed to both Croat emigres and, most predominantly, peasants. In this respect he filled the space of the Croatian Peasant Party led by Radić and then Maček. In 1933, in *Principles of the Ustaše Movement*, Pavelić wrote, "The peasantry is not just the base and source of our life but alone contains the essence of the Croatian people and is, as such, the executive of all state power in the Croatian state." As a result, Pavelić could recruit ordinary Croats to his cause.

At the same time, he also kept links with other underground groups and it was to them he turned to initiate his most incendiary move against the Yugoslav state to date. Pavelić eventually contacted the Macedonian IMRO to plot the assassination of King Alexander I. Having settled on a plan, the IMRO assassins, led by Vlado Chernozemski and backed up by Croats, traveled through Hungary to Switzerland to France, where the king was due to attend a state visit as part of his country's Little Entente agreement. On October 9, 1934, King Alexander I arrived in Marseille, France and began his visit accompanied by the French Foreign Minister through the city in an open car. Chernozemski appeared from the crowd and shot the king twice, killing him.

Communism, Fascism, and World War II

King Alexander I's death shocked a Yugoslav public already disturbed by decades of violence, and 500,000 attended Alexander's funeral. The monarchy then passed to Alexander's son, Peter II, but since he was only 11 years old, power transferred to a regent. Alexander's cousin, Prince Paul, was a far more conciliatory figure than Alexander, relaxing censorship and the political strictures of the dictatorship period. He attempted to reform the country from 1934, in particular, by offering Croats more autonomy.[45] Paul was described as a Yugoslav ruler, rather than adhering to the pro-Serb outlook of his predecessors, but even his more relaxed approach could not satisfy the growing animosity between Serbs and Croats. In fact, the promise of more autonomy only managed to increase the squabbling between Yugoslavia's two largest nationalities.

---

[44] Misha Glenny, *The Balkans 1804-2012: Nationalism, War and the Great Powers* (London: Granta, 2012), p. 433.
[45] David Owen, *Balkan Odyssey* (London: Indigo, 1996), p. 8.

Prince Paul

Peter II

In 1938 Paul appointed a Prime Minister, Dragiša Cvetković, and then the following year, he made Vladko Maček Vice Premier in a final attempt to resolve the tension between Croats and Serbs. Elections were held in 1938 and won by the Yugoslav Radical Union with 54% of the vote, while Maček's United Opposition Party received 45%. In August 1939, the Cvetković–Maček Agreement was signed, forming a Croatian *banovina* with greater autonomy and powers.

Ultimately, it would be to no avail, because Yugoslavia was hurtling towards nationalist violence and authoritarianism far worse than anything the country had experienced in its short history.

The politics of Europe changed rapidly during the 1930s. Many countries abandoned democracy while political parties, and voters, moved towards the extremes of fascism and communism. In Yugoslavia this trend was particularly fraught due to the many different nationalities. A shift to fascist politics was likely to pose problems for ethnic, religious and national minorities. Meanwhile, a charismatic socialist named Josip Broz, now known as Tito, was making his ways through the ranks of the Yugoslav Communist Party.

Yugoslavia had come into existence, in geopolitical terms, through support from the major democratic powers at the end of the First World War. Britain and France, and to a lesser extent the United States, had been strong supporters of the South Slav state idea.[46] The Americans, however, had moved to an isolationist foreign policy after the incapacitation of President Wilson. Washington even failed to support the League of Nations in Geneva despite the institution being the brainchild of Wilson himself. Nevertheless, Britain and France still attempted to back the post-Versailles internationalist world order they had constructed well into the 1920s. Democracy, sovereignty and self-determination were the keystones of this order.

The Wall Street Crash destroyed more than the world's financial system, because the Great Depression upended the political arrangements in many countries. The downturn led to extreme insecurity, in terms of income, jobs, and even food, while authoritarian politicians offered stability, even at the cost of political suppression. As politics in much of Europe drifted towards the extremes of fascism and communism, dictatorships emerged across the continent. Many of these regimes would exploit class or ethnic divisions as tools of consolidating or sustaining their power, and this created unique dangers for a number of countries, particularly those with significant ethnic or religious minorities. The Treaty of Versailles, despite its noble intentions, had redrawn the barriers of a post-imperial Europe and included numerous linguistic, religious and national minorities within a new "nation-state." In the hands of a strongman, like Adolf Hitler, these minorities could be exploited to suit a wider agenda. The large German-speaking minority of Czechoslovakia, for instance, was invoked as a reason for territorial annexation, and the Jewish minority within Germany itself was remorselessly persecuted and characterized as outsiders who did not fit the Nazis' views of eugenics and "racial purity."

The same trends were observed in Yugoslavia. King Alexander I's abandonment of democracy caused a loss of support from Britain and France as liberals in these democracies concluded that the Balkan states had inherent authoritarian tendencies.[47] At the same time, ethnic rivalries

---

[46] Eugene Michail, 'Western Attitudes to War in the Balkans and the Shifting Meanings of Violence, 1912-1991', *Journal of Contemporary History*, (47:219, 2012, pp. 219-241), p. 230.
[47] Ibid, p. 231.

increased over the decade, particularly between Serbs and Croats. In many ways, the trends of the 1930s were uniquely dangerous when applied to Yugoslavia since the country was a fragile multiethnic state already beset with national rivalries. It was even more vulnerable to the forces of violent ethno-nationalism than its contemporaries. In fact, Yugoslavia would experience both extremes, with fascism in power during the Second World War and communism taking root after 1945.

The Little Entente alliance of Yugoslavia, Czechoslovakia and Romania was still in operation during the 1930s. Its "Treaty of Friendship," initially signed in 1922, was extended in 1927, 1932, and 1937. The pooled weight of the initiative, however, proved too weak to resist the more powerful countries. Czechoslovakia was dismantled by the Nazis in 1938 and 1939, and with that the Little Entente no longer functioned. Moreover, the democratic powers, Britain and France, abandoned Czechoslovakia at the 1938 Munich Conference. The Allies were desperate to avoid another continental war with Germany, but also there was some sympathy to German claims that the Treaty of Versailles had imposed unfair conditions on the country and marginalized many ethnic Germans. If Britain and France were willing to disengage with Czechoslovakia, they were likely to do the same with Yugoslavia, particularly as Belgrade had eschewed democracy in 1929.

Once it was clear that these friends would not come to the aid of its allies, Yugoslavia was left exposed to interference from the fascist states. In Yugoslavia, however, it was the Italian threat that most concerned its rulers. By the end of the decade, Belgrade was becoming increasingly concerned about its geopolitical position and security. As a result, Belgrade sought alliances to secure its status, and unfortunately, Prince Paul decided to approach Nazi Germany as a potential protector.[48] Back in 1934, Hermann Göring had attended King Alexander I's funeral and offered the country its diplomatic support. Göring had promised, "Germany will never support any activity…that aims at the break-up of Yugoslavia."[49] These words were to prove wholly false.

Prince Paul visited Hitler in 1939 to garner support for his fragile state, as well as to pay his compliments to the Europe's most powerful leader. Paul's visit appeared to have paid off, and he now felt more secure in the dangerous geopolitical environment. That year, German troops marched into Czechoslovakia and annexed the rest of the territory left over from the 1938 Munich Conference. In September, Germany invaded Poland, which instigated a response from Britain and France and started World War II.

Initially, it appeared that Yugoslavia might somehow be insulated from the conflict despite the dangerous friendship Ante Pavelić had with Benito Mussolini and the Ustaše's activities. After all, Göring and then Hitler had apparently given Paul security assurances, and Yugoslavia had declared its neutrality in 1939 despite the fact Paul was favourable to the Allies, assisting both

---

[48] Brendan Simms, *Europe: The Struggle for Supremacy 1453 to the Present* (London: Penguin, 2014), p. 358.
[49] Misha Glenny, *The Balkans 1804-2012: Nationalism, War and the Great Powers* (London: Granta, 2012), p. 436.

Greece and France in the face of the fascist powers.

However, the situation quickly changed. The Nazis overran Belgium and France in the summer of 1940 and suddenly controlled most of Europe. Hitler's plans and ambitions then turned east, and in 1941 he had the Soviet Union in his sights. Yugoslavia, despite his earlier promises, would become a pawn in a far larger conflagration.

With Nazi power at its zenith, the fascist powers turned their attention to the Balkans in early 1941. They did this through the vehicle of the "Tripartite Pact," an agreement that unified Germany, Japan and Italy the Axis Powers in September 1940. Later that, year a number of countries had joined the pact, including Hungary and Romania, and in March 1941, Bulgaria joined.

Yugoslavia was coerced into signing the Tripartite Pact on March 25, 1941 in Vienna. In fact, Yugoslavia had been in talks – under duress – with the fascist powers for months. Prince Paul had met Hitler at the beginning of March 1941, and Hitler hoped to neutralize the Balkans before he attacked the Soviet Union. He was also worried that Paul was a British stooge. Paul, on the other hand, ultimately agreed to the arrangement because he knew his country had no other reliable allies and he believed signing the pact might prolong Yugoslavia's autonomy. Prime Minister Dragiša Cvetković believed he had secured non-interference in Yugoslavia's affairs in return for the signing of the pact.[50]

As the 1930s constantly proved, assurances from Hitler and the Nazis were utterly worthless, and promises were abrogated through pretexts for military aggression. Yugoslavia's security may have seemed to have been reinforced by joining the Tripartite Pact, but within a matter of weeks, the country would be attacked by the Nazis and dismembered. On March 27, two days after the signing, Prince Paul was overthrown in a military coup with apparent British support. Demonstrators had come out onto the streets of Belgrade the previous day. The coup plotters, based in the Yugoslav Air Force, were also enraged by the signing of the Tripartite Pact and deposed Prince Paul and Prime Minister Cvetković. In their place the plotters installed the assassinated Alexander's son Peter, crowned as King Peter II. The new regime was pro-British and also supported by the Communist Party. At the same time, the coup was deemed as Serb-led and alarmed nationalities outside of the Serb heartlands.

There was also widespread anxiety that the coup would trigger war, and this is precisely what happened. When the new Yugoslav government refused to ratify the Tripartite Pact, it infuriated the Nazis, and Hitler issued the so-called "Directive 25." German forces attacked both Greece and Yugoslavia on April 6, 1941. The Luftwaffe bombed Belgrade for three days, and troops – in conjunction with Hungarian, Romanian and Italian forces – assaulted Yugoslavia from the

---

[50] Blanka Matkovich, *Croatia and Slovenia at the End and After the Second World War (1944-1945): Mass Crimes and Human Rights Violations Committed by the Communist Regime*, (Brown Walker Press, 2017), p. 30.

ground. The Yugoslav army was hopelessly outnumbered, poorly equipped and ill-prepared for aggression on this scale. It capitulated within a matter of days.[51]

The invading countries all wanted a piece of Yugoslavia's territory, and meanwhile, Ustaše leader Ante Pavelić declared an independent state of Croatia on April 10, 1941 while the fighting was still ongoing. The Yugoslav high command then surrendered unconditionally on April 18.

Under the aegis of Hitler, Yugoslavia was dismembered in a fashion to satisfy some of the claims of the Axis. Slovenia was divided and occupied by Germany and Italy, while Serbia was solely occupied by the Nazis. Bulgaria, under Boris III, was given Macedonia, and a puppet regime was installed in Montenegro. Italy claimed Kosovo, the region in the south of Serbia with a majority ethnic Albanian population, and Mussolini had already annexed Albania. Vojvodina, in the north of Serbia, was divided between Hungary and Germany. Finally, and most consequently, Pavelić's Independent Croatian State was recognized, including most of Bosnia and Herzegovina. The Nazis initially offered Maček the leadership of an independent Croatia, but he refused, instructing Croats to support the new state instead. Having spent most of the 1930s agitating for Croatian autonomy as well as organizing Ustaše terrorism, Pavelić had finally achieved his objective of a separate state. Although his Croatia was believed to be a fascist puppet of Italy and Germany, Pavelić would prove able to implement policies of his own accord.

Once the Nazis had pacified the Balkan region, they felt confident enough to invade the Soviet Union in the summer of 1941. In the former Yugoslavia, however, the new Croat regime wasted no time implementing its own version of fascism. Ante Pavelić took the position of *Poglavnik*, essentially a Croatian version of dictator, and set in motion a shocking set of ethno-nationalist policies. Pavelić met Hitler on several occasions during the war, including for the first time in Bavaria in June 1941, and it is believed that the German dictator gave his Croatian counterpart a lot of advice on how to run an effective fascist regime. Pavelić proved to be a faithful student of the Führer - he adorned himself with the usual fascist paraphernalia, including the military uniform, and also took to using the Nazi salute. The Zagreb regime also attempted to create a cult of personality around Pavelić.

The independent state of Croatia that existed between 1941 and 1945 was commonly known by the acronym NDH (*Nezavisna Država Hrvatska* in Serbo-Croat) and was essentially an Italian and German client. Nevertheless, the dictatorship of Ante Pavelić committed countless crimes against those within the territory he controlled.[52] It is estimated that as many as 700,000 people were killed in the NDH during this period, including ethnic Serbs and Jews, Roma, and Croats who opposed the regime. The methods used and the ideology which underpinned the crimes were chillingly similar to the Nazis. The Pavelić regime set up a secret service, the Ustaše

---

[51] The History Channel, '1941: Yugoslavia joins the Axis', (A&E Networks, 2009), https://www.history.com/this-day-in-history/yugoslavia-joins-the-axis, [accessed 21 August 2018]

[52] Ivo Goldstein, 'The Independent State of Croatia in 1941: On the Road to Catastrophe', *Totalitarian Movements and Political Religions*, 7:4, 2006, pp. 417-427.

Intelligence Service, which was charged with rooting out potential "enemies" of the state. A parliament was formed and met in 1942, but it rarely convened afterwards. Power within the NDH was concentrated in the hands of Pavelić and his Ustaše cronies.

The Nazi observers – representatives of one of history's most barbaric regimes – were themselves shocked by the extent of the violence in the NDH. The Nazis demanded that Pavelić implement anti-Semitic policies, which the NDH duly agreed to, but its primary focus was ethnically cleansing their state of Serbs. Pavelić was a racist and an ultra-nationalist who believed that Croatia needed to purge its Serbs, either through deportation, murder, or conversion to Catholicism.[53] Pavelić also installed lieutenants with predilections for extreme violence, such as head of the secret service, Eugen "Dido" Kvaternik, who was described as "bloodthirsty." The Slana death camp was quickly set up on the island of Pag, and then came the Jadovno camp. The majority of the prisoners were Serbs or Jews. The largest camp, however, would be built at Jasenovac, in the Croatian interior.[54] It was here, known as the "Auschwitz of the Balkans," that hundreds of thousands of people lost their lives. As historian Misha Glenny put it, it was not just the numbers but the ferocity of the killing in the NDH that put the Croatian Ustaše in its own vicious category. "Its (the NDH's) uniqueness lay in its brutality."[55] Jasenovac was described as a "slaughterhouse," where inmates could be bludgeoned to death with hammers, where humiliation and torture were endemic, and hygiene was so poor that diseases such as typhus were common.[56] Jasenovac was only the largest of many camps.

[53] Misha Glenny, *The Balkans 1804-2012: Nationalism, War and the Great Powers* (London: Granta, 2012), p. 498.
[54] David Owen, *Balkan Odyssey* (London: Indigo, 1996), p. 9.
[55] Misha Glenny, *The Balkans 1804-2012: Nationalism, War and the Great Powers* (London: Granta, 2012), p. 501.
[56] Ibid, p. 501.

A picture of Serbs being forced to convert to Catholicism

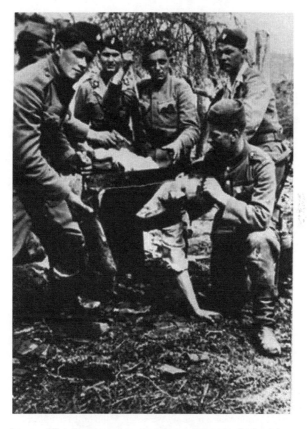

A picture of Ustaše members preparing to behead a Serb with a saw

Pavelić passed a decree in 1941 making all Jews, Serbs, and Roma "non-citizens" of the NDH. Croatia was therefore both active and complicit in the Holocaust. In 1930, around 856,000 Jewish people lived in the Balkans, and just 20 years later that number had fallen to less than 50,000 because of the genocide.[57] In the NDH, almost all Jews were killed during the war - a post-war Yugoslav report stated that out of the 30,000 Jews who lived in the NDH, only 1,500 survived. The Ustaše also targeted the Roma population, with about 30,000 being murdered in the NDH.

The status of Bosnian Muslims, ruled by the NDH from 1941-1945, was more ambiguous. The Ustaše state saw Bosnian Muslims as Croats of the Muslim faith, that is to say ethnically, if not

---

[57] Mark Mazower, *The Balkans: From the End of Byzantium to the Present Day* (London: Phoenix, 2001), p. 125.

religiously, homogeneous. Some Bosnian Muslims collaborated with the Croats in their campaign of ethnic cleansing, while some were victims themselves of NDH state violence.[58] Others, however, resisted the Ustaše and participated in the Partisan movement. Grotesque violence and ethnic cleansing also took place in the occupied zones of Serbia, Slovenia, and others.

By the summer of 1944, the Axis powers were having serious difficulties in the war. The United States and its allies had successfully landed in France and were rapidly driving back German forces there. The Soviets had also started to overrun the Nazis and were making quick progress as they pushed west. Other forces, also led by the United States, were driving back the fascists from the Mediterranean, and Italy had already capitulated. The existence of the NDH was now in the balance, and Zagreb was becoming wary of its fate should the Axis be defeated. Croatia was in jeopardy of occupation by either the democratic Allies or the communist Soviets, and it was understood that neither would be friendly towards the fascist ethno-nationalism of the Pavelić regime.

As a result of this growing uncertainty, the Foreign Minister, Mladen Lorković, and the Minister for War, Ante Vokić, attempted to overthrow Pavelić in a coup in August 1944. The attempt failed and the two men were executed. It was not until May 1945 that the NDH was finally toppled, with its leadership, including the *Poglavnik*, fleeing into exile. Ante Pavelić would spend the rest of his life on the run, eventually taking refuge in Franco's Spain, where he died in 1959.

The Revitalization of Yugoslavia

There were two main strands of resistance to occupation, fascism, and the NDH during the war: monarchists (or "Chetniks") and communists (or "Partisans"). The terror of the Ustaše drove many, particularly Serbs, into the ranks of both sides.[59] The Chetniks were led by Draža Mihailović, an officer in the Yugoslav army who took to the hills with other resistance fighters after the occupation of Serbia. Chetnik forces initiated low-level fighting against the occupying forces, as well as other groups within Yugoslavia such as the Ustaše and Bosnian Muslims. The ultimate aim of the Chetniks was to form a Greater Serbia, in the Balkan tradition of the "Megali Idea," and the Chetniks were committed to reinstating the Karađorđević monarchy. The Chetniks provided the most significant resistance to the Germans in 1941, and this was reflected in the international backing they achieved. Mihailović made radio broadcasts expressing support for the exiled King Peter II and attempted to garner support from the Allies, such as Britain.

---

[58] David Owen, *Balkan Odyssey* (London: Indigo, 1996), p. 8.
[59] Misha Glenny, *The Balkans 1804-2012: Nationalism, War and the Great Powers* (London: Granta, 2012), p. 486.

Mihailović

The other main group was led by Tito, who had risen up the ranks of the Communist Party during the 1930s. Tito was born in Croatia in 1892 to a Croat mother and a Slovene father. He had joined the Communist Party shortly after the First World War and had been an underground revolutionary during the 1920s after the party was banned by the Yugoslav government. He later served time in prison and then went into exile. After spending time in the Soviet Union working for the Cominterm (the Communist International organisation) and recruiting fighters for the Spanish Civil War, Tito was appointed General Secretary of the Yugoslav Communist Party in 1937. When Yugoslavia was invaded and divided in April 1941, Tito organized a small band of communist fighters to take to the Montenegrin mountains and launch operations against both the Nazis and the Ustaše.

In 1941, Tito worked alongside Mihailović, and the two groups had some success when they liberated an area of western Serbia which they dubbed the Republic of Užice, but the Germans retook the area at the end of 1941 and Tito's Partisans fled to Bosnia and Herzegovina. The shift of support of the Allies from the Chetniks to the Partisans indicates how much more effective Tito's forces were, in particular in terms of propaganda, in comparison to Mihailović. It was also a critical moment in the development of Yugoslavia once the war was over. Tito saw the war as an opportunity to bring Yugoslavia over to his communist cause, as well as to achieve a position of supremacy over other groups such as the Chetniks. Tito was therefore astute in his temporary alliances, always keen not to engage in too much heavy fighting that could potentially destroy the basis of his worker's state.

Meanwhile, King Peter II was supported by the Allies and had lived in Britain during his exile. As a result, Britain initially backed the monarchist fighters within Yugoslavia - the Chetniks - and their leader Draža Mihailović. It became clear, however, that Tito's Partisans were the more effective resistance to the fascists, particularly as the Chetniks were proving sectarian in their attacks on other Yugoslav nationalities. In 1943, British Prime Minister Winston Churchill changed his policy towards Yugoslavia and decided to back Tito.[60] Churchill had visited Cairo in January 1943 and received intelligence reports from SOE (Special Operations Executive) about the situation in Yugoslavia, although the accuracy of the reports was later contested. Indeed, there were allegations after the war that operatives sympathetic to communism in the foreign office exaggerated the role and reputation of the Partisans and downplayed those of the Chetniks.

In any case, Churchill's shift towards Tito would have a profound impact on the region. Churchill instructed his agents to make contact with Tito and the Partisans shortly after his trip to Cairo. A number of British messengers visited Tito, and Churchill then assigned a special envoy, Fitzroy Maclean, to liaise with the Partisans. Churchill then informed President Roosevelt of his change in policy at the 1943 Tehran Conference. The British had wildly overestimated the Partisan strength, but it meant they provided the Partisans with military aid and diplomatic support, thereby isolating Mihailović. Churchill then sought to meet the elusive Tito, finally meeting him in person in Italy in August 1944.

It is perhaps surprising that the British – particularly the anti-communist Churchill – would support Tito and his communist Partisans during the war, but the British had convinced themselves that the Partisans were their best bet for defeating the Nazis.[61] Secondly, the British were consistently supporters of the status quo in the Balkans and may have believed that the communists presented the best opportunity for stability and could bind together Yugoslavia's various factions.

By the end of 1944, it was clear that the war was in its final phase, and the focus within the

---

[60] Christopher Catherwood, *Churchill and Tito: SOE, Bletchley Park and Supporting the Yugoslav Communists in World War II* (Frontline Books, 2017)
[61] David Binder, 'A Coffin for Mihailović', *New York Times*, 10 February 1991, https://www.nytimes.com/1991/02/10/books/a-coffin-for-mihailovic.html, [accessed 21 August 2018]

country itself turned towards what would happen after the war was over. Tito had formed the National Committee for the Liberation of Yugoslavia (NKOJ) in late 1943, while the competing royalists, headed by King Peter II in London, had formed a separate government-in-exile. Ivan Šubašić, the nominated Prime Minister of the latter, eventually made an agreement with Tito to unite the two factions over the course of the second half of 1944. King Peter II and Šubašić, who headed the Croatia *banovina* before the war, were essentially recognising Tito as the ultimate representative of the Yugoslav people.

With these agreements, however, Mihailović and the Chetniks were excluded from the post-fascist power structure. Among other things, the Tito-Šubašić agreements, which were championed by Churchill, supposedly meant that post-war Yugoslavia would be governed as a democracy and a federation of the different nationalities. Mihailović was further marginalized as the Chetniks were accused of having collaborated with the Axis.

In early 1945, Germany still occupied Yugoslavia, but its power was hanging on by a thread. The Partisans launched a General Offensive in March and managed to occupy several pieces of territory outside Yugoslavia, including Trieste in Italy, as well as parts of Austria. Tito's forces, supported by the Soviet Red Army, also overran the NDH. The Ustaše retreated into Austria but surrendered in May 1945.

With the Germans and Ustaše now out of Yugoslavia, King Peter II re-entered the picture as titular head of state. Tito was opposed, however, to the continuation of the Karađorđević monarchy, and the situation was ambiguous in mid-1945 despite Tito giving the impression he had endorsed the king's position. Post-war elections were subsequently held on November 11, 1945. Tito was backed by the "People's Front" and gained an unlikely 90.5% of the vote. The king and his "Regency Council" accepted Tito's position as Prime Minister.

Following this decision, Tito's socialist committee, the Constituent Assembly, deposed the king, who fled into exile in the United States. The Federal People's Republic of Yugoslavia was founded on November 29, 1945, and Yugoslavia now entered a new era after the nightmare of the war years and the occupation and crimes of the Nazis and the Ustaše. Moving forward, Yugoslavia would be a socialist federation, led for the most part by Tito. The country would develop its brand of communism that proved more acceptable to the West, which gave Tito substantial financial support.

Nevertheless, Yugoslavia shared many of the characteristics of other communist regimes in Central and Eastern Europe. Tito was ruthless in sidelining his opponents, including going after Mihailović, which demonstrated to the other nationalities that the new Yugoslavia would not be a Greater Serbia. Mihailović went into hiding after the end of the war but was captured in March 1946, convicted of war crimes and treason in a show trial, and executed in July 1946. The animosity that this caused, as well as the suppression of the Chetniks, would resurface in the 1990s, but for the next several decades, Tito would mold Yugoslavia in his own image, and the rest of the state's history would be indelibly linked with the communist leader.

Online Resources

Other books about 20th century history by Charles River Editors

Other books about Tito on Amazon

Bibliography

Badredine Arfi, *International Change and the Stability of Multiethnic States. Yugoslavia, Lebanon, and Crises of Governance.* (Indianapolis: Indiana University Press, 2005)

David Binder, 'A Coffin for Mihailovic', *New York Times*, 10 February 1991, https://www.nytimes.com/1991/02/10/books/a-coffin-for-mihailovic.html

Nada Boskovska, *Yugoslavia and Macedonia Before Tito: Between Repression and Integration* (London: IB Tauris, 2016)

Christopher Catherwood, *Churchill and Tito: SOE, Bletchley Park and Supporting the Yugoslav Communists in World War II* (Frontline Books, 2017)

Dejan Djokić, 'Versailles and Yugoslavia: ninety years on', *Open Democracy*, 26 June 2009, https://www.opendemocracy.net/article/versailles-and-yugoslavia-ninety-years-on

Dejan Djokić, *Pasic & Trumbic: The Kingdom of Serbs, Croats and Slovenes.* (Haus Publishing, 2010)

Vesna Drapac, *Constructing Yugoslavia: A Transnational History*, (Basingstoke: Palgrave Macmillan, 2010)

Richard J. Evans, *The Pursuit of Power: Europe 1815-1914* (London: Penguin, 2017)

Tom Gallagher, *Outcast Europe: The Balkans, 1789-1989: From the Ottomans to Milošević*, (London: Routledge, 2001)

Robert Gerwarth, *The Vanquished: Why the First World War Failed to End, 1917-1923* (London: Allen Lane, 2016)

Ivo Goldstein, 'The Independent State of Croatia in 1941: On the Road to Catastrophe', *Totalitarian Movements and Political Religions*, 7:4, 2006, pp. 417-427

Misha Glenny, *The Balkans 1804-2012: Nationalism, War and the Great Powers* (London: Granta, 2012)

The History Channel, '1941: Yugoslavia joins the Axis', (A&E Networks, 2009),
https://www.history.com/this-day-in-history/yugoslavia-joins-the-axis

Godfrey Hodgson, *People's Century: From the dawn of the century to the eve of the millennium* (Godalming: BBC Books, 1998)

Paul Kennedy, *The Rise and Fall of the Great Powers: Economic Change and Military Conflict from 1500 to 2000* (New York: Random House, 1987)

James M. Lindsay, 'TWE Remembers: Austria-Hungary Issues an Ultimatum to Serbia', *Council on Foreign Relations*, 23 July 2014, https://www.cfr.org/blog/twe-remembers-austria-hungary-issues-ultimatum-serbia

Sonia Lucarelli, *Europe and the Breakup of Yugoslavia. A Political Failure in Search of a Scholarly Explanation*, (The Hague: Kluwer Law International, 2000)

Oto Luthar (ed), *The Land Between: A History of Slovenia* (Frankfurt am Main: Peter Lang, 2008)

Blanka Matkovich, *Croatia and Slovenia at the End and After the Second World War (1944-1945): Mass Crimes and Human Rights Violations Committed by the Communist Regime*, (Brown Walker Press, 2017)

Mark Mazower, *The Balkans: From the End of Byzantium to the Present Day* (London: Phoenix, 2001)

Eugene Michail, 'Western Attitudes to War in the Balkans and the Shifting Meanings of Violence, 1912-1991', *Journal of Contemporary History*, (47:219, 2012), 219-241.

Eugene Michail, *The British and the Balkans. Forming Images of Foreign Lands, 1900-1950.* (London: Continuum, 2011)

David Owen, *Balkan Odyssey* (London: Indigo, 1996)

Laura Silber and Allan Little, *The Death of Yugoslavia* (London: Penguin, 1996)

Brendan Simms, *Europe: The Struggle for Supremacy 1453 to the Present* (London: Penguin, 2014)

Brendan Simms, *Unfinest Hour: Britain and the Destruction of Bosnia*, (London: Penguin, 2001)

Free Books by Charles River Editors

We have brand new titles available for free most days of the week. To see which of our titles are currently free, click on this link.

Discounted Books by Charles River Editors

We have titles at a discount price of just 99 cents everyday. To see which of our titles are currently 99 cents, click on this link.

Made in the USA
Las Vegas, NV
14 December 2023

82772549R00031